The Legacy Of SEDONA SCHNEBLY

AUTHOR KATE RULAND-THORNE

Dedicated to Clara and Margaret,
daughters of Carl and Sedona Schnebly,
without whose help and encouragement
the true story of their parents would
never have been told, and to my
good friend, artist Susan Kliewer,
who has captured the essence and spirit of
Sedona Miller Schnebly so eloquently
in her monumental bronze statue of
Sedona - the first work of art to be
donated to the City of Sedona by the
Red Rocks Arts Council for its
Art in Public Places program.

THORNE Enterprises
Publications, Inc.

SEDONA BOOKS & MUSIC
140 Coffee Pot Drive, Ste E-103-A
Sedona, Arizona 86336
(520) 203-0711

I

CREDITS

Editor   Aliza Caillou
Cover Design & Graphics   Ron Henry Design
Kleiwer/Schnebly Biography   Lisa Schnebly
(Great-granddaughter of Carl and Sedona Schnebly)
Reprinted from an article in the Sedona Magazine and
Visitors' Guide, Fall 1994, with permission from the
author and the publisher.
Printer   Millenia Graphics
            Colorado Springs, CO
Photo Credit   Charlotte Schnebly Parker

Second Printing, 1999

ISBN #09628329-9-5

Sedona Arabella Miller Schnebly
Born: Gorin, Missouri
February 24, 1877
Died: Sedona, Arizona
November 13, 1950

Sedona Miller, *1890's*
Photo courtesy of Paula Schnebly Hokanson

s far as Sedona Miller Schnebly's father was concerned, she had no business running off to Indian Territory with that infernal husband of hers, Carl. As a last resort, Philip Miller issued a warning. "If you go," he said, "I'll write you out of my will." Sedona went, and Philip Miller made good his threat.

How wrenching it must have been to defy her father and move away from her family and friends in Gorin, Missouri, the town of her birth. How terrified she must have felt arriving with her two small children in the wild and raucous mining town of Jerome. There Carl, who had gone ahead two weeks before, met them at the train and took them by wagon over a rough road into an uncivilized unknown.

What were Sedona Schnebly's thoughts and feelings when Carl showed her the land he had bought along the banks of Oak Creek? Did she thrill to the jagged walls of red rock that surrounded her, or did they overpower her and fill her with fear? There was no home to live in when she arrived. That would have to be built later. She must make do with an old run down bunkhouse and later a tent.

But Carl Schnebly was filled with plans and dreams, and they were infectious. Together they would show Philip Miller how wrong he had been. Besides, Sedona loved Carl Schnebly with all of her being. She had married him over her father's objections, and now she had no choice but to follow him wherever he went. His dreams became her dreams. Together they would make something of this land, something they would be proud of. And in time, with prayers, hard work and lots of luck, they would succeed.

The year was 1901 when the Schneblys arrived at their new home. There were untold adjustments for Sedona to make. Always before, she had sisters to share her feelings with and a mother to turn to when she needed advice. Now there was only Carl and her two babies, Elsworth and Pearl. The loneliness must have been terrible, quite like the loneliness experienced by so many other pioneer wives who wrote often of it in their diaries and letters.

Then too, there was so much work to be done and without any conveniences to lighten the load. There was no store nearby, no post office. Neighbors lived far away, and doctors were almost non-existent. But Sedona Schnebly was made of strong stuff. Although she had been raised in a wealthy home by prominent parents, she knew how to work, she knew how to cook and she knew how to make the best of things.

Sedona Arabella Miller was the sixth child and second daughter born to a Pennsylvania Dutch couple, Philip and Amanda Miller. The Millers had five more daughters and another son after Sedona was born, but none of their other eleven children was given a more unusual name. When asked later why she gave her daughter this name, Amanda Miller explained that she had never heard the name before, she simply made it up. "After all, there is a first time for any name or word," she said.

Sedona's father, Philip Miller, was the second largest landowner in the Gorin area. His farm stretched toward the nearby town of Edna. When Sedona was born, Gorin was not yet a town. In fact it was called Octavia then and was merely a collection of farms made up of pasture, timberland and rough horse trails. Mail was deposited in leather pouches tacked up and down an old elm tree. It was from around this elm tree that the town of Gorin eventually sprouted.

About one mile east of this elm tree, a little log cabin served as a schoolhouse. For awhile it also served as a church on Sundays for the three predominant religions of the area: Methodist, Baptist and Presbyterian. The Millers were staunch Methodists, a matter that would affect Sedona's life twenty years later when she met, and then defied her father by marrying, Theodore Carleton (T.C.) Schnebly. Carl Schnebly was an equally staunch 'predestination' Presbyterian.

When Sedona was ten years old, the Atchison, Topeka, and Santa Fe Railroad Company began construction of a division of their road from Kansas City to Chicago. Gorin, located in the northern corner of Missouri, lay right in the path the railroad planned to cross. When the railroad executives arrived to obtain land right-of-ways on which to lay their track, they liberally paid one Philip Miller for the use of much of the land they needed.

By 1887, the first train finally passed through Gorin, and hundreds of people flocked to the tracks to see the sight. Most had never seen a train before. Unquestionably, the Miller family was in full attendance.

After the railroad came, a building boom followed and Gorin, Missouri, was officially incorporated as a town in 1887. The post office was moved inside a building and Philip Miller eventually served as Gorin's fourth postmaster.

Along the railroad tracks, a grist mill and a flour mill sprang up, and near the depot a pickle factory opened. The farmers who raised wheat and cucumbers prospered. Philip Miller was one of them.

But despite all the prosperity that the town, or Philip Miller and his family enjoyed, the Miller children were expected to live by the Protestant work ethic and work in the fields on the family farm. The Miller children did not live a pampered life but one that was structured, genteel and imbued with solid Methodist teachings.

Sedona was rarely called by her given name. Throughout her life, family and friends called her "Dona." When she was small, some even referred to her as "that little pop-eyed Donie Miller."

Although Dona's life was a simple one, Philip Miller did believe in educating his children. Dona and her siblings were sent to a private finishing school, the Gorin Academy. All spoke German as fluently as they did English, and we know Sedona had elocution, piano and organ lessons.

After finishing her own education, Sedona taught school for awhile. Then at some point before her 20th birthday, she met her future husband, Carl.

Theodore Carleton Schnebly was born near Hagerstown, Maryland, on December 29, 1868. He was the fourth of twelve children born to Daniel

Henry, Jr., and Maria Elizabeth Davis Schnebly. Carl's family moved to Kahoka, Missouri, when he was still a small boy. Carl's close-knit family were devout Presbyterians. All worked hard on their family farm, too. When Carl and his four brothers graduated from high school, each earned degrees at Kahoka College. Like Philip and Amanda Miller, the Schnebly family descended from Pennsylvania Dutch stock.

The term 'Pennsylvania Dutch' was coined by early English colonists who really meant to say 'Deutsh,' meaning German. The term soon became corrupted to mean Dutch. It was a name applied to those Germans and Swiss who migrated by the thousands to America in the 1700's and who settled primarily in south-central and eastern Pennsylvania and in Maryland.

Carl's great-grandfather, Dr. Henirich Schnebly, emigrated from Zurich, Switzerland, to America in 1750 at the age of 22. Shortly after he arrived in America, he became very ill. When he finally recovered, all of his savings were gone and he had to walk from New York to Washington County, Maryland, where many of his Swiss companions had settled. Through skill, industry and the practice of medicine, "Dr. Henry" eventually acquired an enormous tract of land called the "Garden of Eden," five miles north of Hagerstown, Maryland, where Carl was born. When Dr. Henry died at the age of 77, he was one of the largest landholders in Washington County. He also owned vast tracts of land in Kentucky and West Virginia.

Dr. Henry and his first wife Elizabeth Snavely had four sons, Henry, John, Jacob and David and a daughter, Elizabeth. He had no children by his second wife Catherine Wetsol. Dr. Henry left a farm to each grandchild who was named after him, hence a family genealogy rife with the name Henry. Theodore Carleton's father, Daniel Henry, Jr., very likely was one of Dr. Henry's fortunate grandchildren.

By 1894, Carl Schnebly and three of his four brothers, William, Jacob, and Elsworth, had formed a partnership in a hardware store in Gorin, Missouri. It was about this time that Carl began to court Sedona Miller. Despite the fact that Carl and Sedona shared the same Pennsylvania Dutch roots, that Carl descended from a prominent family, and that he was an established businessman with a college education, Philip Miller neither liked nor approved of Carl's courtship with his daughter and tried to dissuade her from seeing him.

"Why," he must have nagged Sedona, "don't you find a nice young man like Loring Johnson?" Loring Johnson was a charming, handsome man who owned a clothing business. While Carl was courting Sedona, Loring was courting Sedona's sister, Lillie Victoria. Both young couples planned their weddings in the same year. The big plus for Loring, as far as Philip Miller, was concerned was that Loring was a Methodist. A common wag among the town gossips at that time was that Philip Miller was getting 100 sons-in-law. "Loring was one and Carl was double zeros."

Over her father's objections, Sedona Arabella married Carl Schnebly on her 20th birthday, February 24, 1897, and six months later, Lillie Victoria married Loring Johnson. Years later, to the horror of the family, and the town of Gorin, Loring Johnson was convicted of embezzlement and served time in both Leavenworth and San Quentin Prisons.

When each of Philip Miller's children married,

he built them a new home as a wedding gift. There is some indication that this was not offered to Sedona and Carl, or perhaps Carl refused the offer. One thing is certain, Carl was giving serious consideration to moving his family away from Gorin and into 'Indian country.' It was a decision which caused the final break with Philip, who threatened to write Sedona out of his will if she and Carl went through with their plans.

But Carl's brother Elsworth whose health was poor, had already gone to Arizona Territory in 1898 in the hope that a better climate might bring about better health. Elsworth found his way into the red rock country of north central Arizona, bought a burro, a bed roll and a camp outfit and for the next few years, hunted and fished up and down Oak Creek Canyon. As Elsworth's health improved, he regularly wrote to his brothers extolling the virtues of this magnificent country and urging them to join him.

In the fall of 1901, Carl decided to act upon his brother's suggestion, and Philip Miller made good his threat to write his daughter out of his will.

On October 12, 1901, Carl Schnebly arrived in Jerome Junction, Arizona Territory via Flagstaff on a Santa Fe "emigrant" train. One car of the train was loaded with all the family possessions including furniture, farm equipment and a team of horses. Carl had no choice but to leave everything but his horses on the side of the mountain for awhile until he could retrieve them. Carl was assured by a member of the Farley family (who later became Sedona residents) that everything would remain safe. Eleven days later, Sedona and the Schneblys' two children, Elsworth, age three and Pearl, age two, also arrived in Jerome. Carl took them by

Philip and
Amanda Miller,
1890's

Sedona and
Carl Schnebly,
1897

Trip Down the Grand Canyon
*1903. Sedona is on third mule
with Carl behind her holding
Genivieve.*

Elsworth, born May 11,
1898, *with his mother.*

Photos courtesy of Paula Schnebly Hokanson

wagon over a rough, rocky, sandy wagon track to their new home.

The family arrived in a place known by some as Upper Oak Creek Crossing and by others as Camp Garden. Those others consisted of about five families. Old J.J. Thompson's family still lived at Indian Gardens. Among the other families were the Armijo and Chavez families and the Schuerman and Dumas families. Most had arrived in the area in the late 1880's.

When Carl finally was able to return to Jerome to retrieve the family goods, he found them intact and undisturbed. He had settled his family on an 80-acre farm which his brother Elsworth had purchased from the Frank Owenby family. On this same land eight decades later, the city of Sedona's famous Los Abrigados Resort would be built.

When the Schneblys first settled on their new land, there was only a bunkhouse on the place for them to live in. Carl planned a large home, but it would take many months of travel back and forth to Flagstaff to collect enough lumber for the project.

In those days, the only way to get to Flagstaff was by following the old Beaver Head stagecoach road. The stage site, located today 11 miles south of Sedona off Hwy. 179, was built in 1876 and abandoned in 1882. In its heyday, the stage carried passengers through the struggling young territory from Prescott to Santa Fe, N.M.

Until 1902, the stage line trail was the only wagon road north out of the Verde Valley. For a loaded wagon, the 60-mile journey took almost a week to travel. After the stage line was abandoned in 1882, the route became known as the Verde Valley Wagon Road.

But Carl soon discovered there were shorter

The Schnebly home, *1902-1907.*

"Tad" (Elsworth) with his
sister Pearl, *1900.*

The Schnebly Family in Sedona
prior to Pearl's death, *1905.*

Photos courtesy of Paula Schnebly Hokanson

routes to Flagstaff. One in particular went straight up a mountain. It was primarily a cattle trail created by a Flagstaff rancher named Munds. Going straight up over the mountain reduced travel time one-way to only two days.

J.J. Thompson had contracted with Coconino County to complete the road, which had been worked on for several years by other pioneer families. It didn't take long for Carl's shrewd business mind to figure out that reducing travel time by several days would allow him to get fresh produce quickly to the lucrative Flagstaff market. According to Coconino County records, Carl and his brother Elsworth were both paid to help the road crew transform the last ten miles of the trail into a usable wagon road which we know today as Schnebly Hill Road.

The Coconino County supervisors approved the road in 1902. Several families in the Verde Valley contributed $300 and Carl added $300 of his own.

The construction crew, which included Carl's brother Elsworth, used only picks and shovels. Whenever the road had to be dynamited, the holes for the dynamite were hand-drilled into the rocks. All the men worked 12 hours a day for $1 a day and stayed on the job for over six months until the road was completed.

In the late summer of 1902, Carl already was trucking produce up the Schnebly Hill Road to Flagstaff. When market-bound, Carl would leave his creek-side home in the late evening and drive to the last level spot between his home and the top of the mountain. There he camped out for the night. After feeding and watering his four horses, he turned two of them loose to go home. By early morning, Carl continued the long, all day journey to Flagstaff. He returned home within three days with lumber for his new home and, later, supplies for his small store. He often brought visitors back to Sedona who camped out in tents on the Schnebly property.

Once completed, the Schneblys' new home was a two-story, eleven-room frame house with a basement that measured 30 x 32 feet. The old bunkhouse was turned over to young Pearl and Elsworth for a playhouse. Elsworth remembered that he and Pearl would pick their father's luscious strawberries and use them to decorate their mud pies after 'baking' them in the old bunkhouse stove.

Before long, the Schnebly home was known as a place where one could stay the night and enjoy a good meal. The Schnebly home was not referred to as a hotel until many years later. A hotel was never the building's original purpose.

The journey between Flagstaff and Jerome was such a long and arduous one that people just naturally wanted to stop over along the way, and the Schneblys owned the only home large enough to accommodate paying guests. In time, the Schneblys also rented tents on their property as more and more people chose to remain. Sedona's reputation as an excellent cook added to people's desire to linger. Guests came often to hunt and fish while others stayed for months seeking to improve their health in the pristine climate. Board and room never exceeded a dollar a day.

One such guest was a reporter, Harry Quimby, of a Boston newspaper, the Union Manchester. In 1903, Quimby filled three full pages of his paper with descriptions of the paradise he had discovered in Arizona and the charming family he stayed with for three weeks, a Mr. Carl Schnebly and his lovely wife, Sedona. Here is an excerpt from his story.

Mr. Schnebly puts most of his efforts in his garden and markets his products in Flagstaff making two trips a week in the busy season. His loads average him $60 a trip and many of them amount to over $100 during the busy season. The prices he gets for his fresh produce would make many a New England housewife resort to the canned variety. He markets nothing less than $5 per hundred: Sweet corn brings 35ᶜ a dozen, tomatoes, 8⅓ᶜ a pound, watermelons 5ᶜ a pound, and cantaloupe, cauliflower and summer squash, 8⅓ᶜ a pound. Berries in very small boxes fetch him 20ᶜ a pound while he gets as high as 8⅓ᶜ a pound for his apples and peaches. Some of these prices are wholesale at that.

Mr. Schnebly also runs a small store here where a visitor can buy bacon, flour or tobacco. By this means, he always has a load both ways on his trips to Flagstaff.

His wife, Sedona, operates a small summer hotel and it is an ideal place to rest and study some of Arizona's finest scenery. Of course Oak Creek Canyon is not to be compared with the Grand Canyon for grandeur, but it surely remind one of that place.

Mr. Schnebly's ranch is also a post office having mail twice a week. It is carried over a star route of 20 miles. I was here on election day and it was surely a quiet election. There were hardly enough permanent voters to fill the offices. There were twelve votes cast, all Democratic.

After only two years from the time of their arrival in the area, it can be said that Carl and Sedona's drive and industry were primarily responsible for turning their little hamlet into something that had the makings of a town. Not only had the Schneblys established the area's first hotel, grocery store, profitable truck farm (and if one wants to stretch it - health spa), Carl housed the first post office and served as the area's first postmaster.

Initially when Carl applied for the first post office, he submitted the names of Oak Creek Crossing and Schnebly Station to the Postmaster General in Washington, D.C. Both names were rejected because the cancellation stamp couldn't handle that many words. It was Elsworth, Carl's brother, who suggested he call the new town Sedona. "Why don't we name it after Dona?" he asked one day during breakfast. Carl seized upon the idea. So at the young age of 25, Sedona Arabella's unusual name was established for posterity, and she became known as the mother of the town. Today, residents can be grateful that Sedona's mother did not give her a more ordinary name like Mildred.

When Goldie Genevieve was born on October 22, 1903, Sedona really had her hands full. With Carl gone most of the time hauling produce back and forth to Flagstaff, the majority of the chores around their ranch were left to her.

Not only did she cook and clean for her family, but for their numerous guests as well. Laundry had to be washed in tubs by the creek. Wearing Carl's overalls, Sedona worked in the garden and helped herd and brand their cattle. Like most pioneer women, Sedona sewed all the family clothes, made her own soap, canned tons of fruits and vegetables and became adept at killing rattlesnakes with a broom handle.

Somehow, she found time to gather her guests and area residents together for an occasional sing-a-long or a non-denominational church service in her home on Sundays. Sometimes a visiting preacher showed up to give a sermon, but most of the time the services consisted of Bible reading and hymn singing with Sedona providing the accompaniment on her prized piano.

By 1904, the Schneblys did hire a Chinese cook. Young Elsworth recalled that the old man did not like cats. Whenever one of the family cats invaded his kitchen, he would threaten to "putee it into the lice soup."

Holidays were particularly special in the Schnebly home. Invitations to their Thanksgiving feasts were prized, so much so that 50 years later, Dr. Ralph Palmer remembered his Thanksgiving dinner with the Schneblys in his book, DOCTOR ON HORSEBACK:

> *On Thanksgiving, we rode to the Schnebly ranch. The Schneblys were sure good providers in the food line. There were some twenty of us at a long table with a haunch of venison at one end and a roasted whole pig at the other. On one side was a turkey and the other a goose, both stuffed and roasted. One of the vegetables which particularly impressed me was a large squash stuffed with cabbage and baked.*

Despite the incredible work load and tremendous responsibilities, Sedona and Carl were happier than they had ever been. Their lives were filled with love, good friends and productivity. Unfortunately, fate intervened, and one day a dreadful tragedy would put an end to their dreams and to their growing prosperity.

On June 12, 1905, Sedona, her son Elsworth, then age seven, and Pearl, age five, were herding milk cows. Sedona held baby Genevieve in the saddle in front of her as she rode. As young as they were, Elsworth and Pearl were already skilled at riding their well-trained, gentle cow ponies.

It was always a pleasant chore to bring in the milk cows each evening, particularly in the early summer when the air was cool and the light from the setting sun gave the red rocks a shimmering, fiery glow. It was one chore Sedona and the children looked forward to. Often on these occasions, she and the children searched for arrowheads or christened rock formations with new and funny names.

But on that particular day, five year-old Pearl, her sun bonnet tied securely around her neck, started down a steep embankment. One story is that she wanted to retrieve an arrow head she had spotted. Childlike, she looped the reins around her neck in order to have her hands free to reach her prize. Seeing this, her mother shouted a warning, but it was too late. A cow suddenly broke from the herd and Pearl's well-trained pony started after it. Pearl wildly clutched at her saddle as the pony pivoted. She was thrown over the pony's neck only to be jerked, trampled and dragged to death as the terrified pony dashed madly toward home.

Elsworth recalled that tragic day many years later and added that it was a sight never to be erased from his memory:

It was a wild and terrifying ride down the banks toward home. Mother frantically urged her horse to go faster while holding on to Genevieve for dear life. Some men working nearby saw Pearl's pony racing home and knew something was wrong. They arrived ahead of Mother and carried the battered body of little Pearl into the house. I picked up one of Pearl's shoes in the doorway.

All that was left of Pearl's clothing was the bonnet strings still tied securely around her neck. The accident was horrible beyond belief for Sedona, who blamed herself. She cut up her lovely wedding dress to make Pearl's shroud. Grandma Thompson, J.J. 's wife, came down from the canyon to help prepare the little girl for burial.

Pearl was buried in the Schnebly's front yard, and every time Sedona looked out her window, she was reminded of that dreadful day. Before long, she began to withdraw into a world of her own, and her once robust health rapidly faded. As Sedona's health continued to decline, the doctors told Carl to move his wife away before her haunting memory took an irreversible toll. Four months later, the Schneblys returned to Gorin, Missouri.

After arriving in Gorin, Carl took a job with the Prairie Oil and Gas Company as a lineman and Sedona made peace with her father, who died of complications during surgery nine months later.

Sedona's youngest sister Pearl, age 18, recently had died also, so the Millers and Schneblys had grief to share. This very likely helped soften Philip Miller's once hardened heart.

After Philip Miller died, the Schneblys left Gorin for Memphis, Missouri, where Carl went into the clothing business with his brother-in-law Loring Johnson. A year later, the Schnebly's second son, Daniel Henry, named for Carl's father, was born on August 22, 1907. The birth of a new baby helped to heal Sedona's broken heart.

Although the partnership with his scheming brother-in-law, Loring, lasted four years, one can only speculate as to whether Carl fell victim to Loring's fraudulent practices. What is apparent is that the Schneblys left Missouri with very little capital to invest when Carl decided to return to farming.

The Schneblys did not return to Arizona because Carl's older brother Elsworth, who could not keep up the prodigious work load on the Schnebly ranch, already had sold it and gone back into teaching. Several years later, the eleven-room ranch house, then owned by the Black family, burned to the ground. The Blacks are the ones who referred to the original Schnebly home as a hotel.

Carl's only chance to own land again was to homestead it, so he moved his family to Boyero, Colorado, where homestead land was still available and where some of their Missouri friends had settled. Carl filed for his first homestead on September 22, 1910. In Boyero, the last of their six children were born: Clara Amanda on January 31, 1912, and Margaret Elizabeth on June 30, 1915. Sedona was 38 years old when Margaret was born.

Clara still has vivid recollections of the Schneblys' life in Boyero, a town of about 100 citizens. Both she and Margaret contributed many insights into her parents' attitudes and personality and described a lifestyle that, it is sad to say, has all but disappeared from the American scene:

Our parents were deeply religious people and saw to it that we went to church every Sunday regardless of the weather, said Clara. In the winter, we took warm bricks to put under our feet while we rode to church in a horse-drawn spring wagon.

Mother and dad were very caring parents and did all they could to make us happy. They were a congenial couple and I personally never remember cross words between them. Margaret reminded me that now and then mother did get provoked with dad, particularly when he got into arguements about religion or politics. On those occasions she threatened to go to live the barn. I never understood why she wanted to go to the barn when our house was so nice.

People were always welcomed into our home, even strangers and if the strangers needed a meal or a place to sleep for the night, our folks provided this for them.

Mother made all of our clothes and dad made new soles for our shoes when they wore out. We each had two pairs of shoes. One for school and one for church.

I never knew where money came from except there was some in a cup in the cupboard which we used for stamps, or other incidentals, but we never had any for anything else.

Mother made candy for us like fudge, divinity and taffy, but I thought store-bought candy was a real treat. It always disturbed me when dad took eggs and cream to the grocery store and traded them for groceries we needed. That way he never owed a bill. Most of the neighbors charged their groceries and

The Schnebly Family
in Gorin, Mo., 1907.

Ellsworth age seven
and Genivieve two,
*taken five months after
Pearl's death, 1905.*

*Photos courtesy of
Paula Schnebly Hokanson*

when they paid their bill, the grocer gave them a bag of candy to take to their children. Dad never got one and that upset me.

Dad forbade dancing, drinking and card playing. He said that if you went to dances there was always drinking and if you drank, it led to gambling. He did allow some card games such as Authors and Flinch, which we played as a family on Sundays or on bad weather days.

Our folks loved to celebrate holidays. At Easter we had scads of colored eggs that we would hunt all day. On the Fourth of July there were plenty of fire crackers, rockets, sparklers, lemonade and homemade ice cream. On Valentine's Day we made our own Valentines using wall paper samples with pretty flowers which we cut from seed catalogs and used to decorate our valentines.

Of course Thanksgiving and Christmas were very special with a big turkey dinner and a house full of guests.

Even though we had little rain in Boyero and hailstorms often destroyed our crops just before harvest time, I never heard dad complain. If a big hailstorm ruined the crops, dad would send us out with buckets after it was over and we would collect hailstones and mother made ice cream with them.

Dad depended on the Farmer's Almanac for just about everything regarding farming. Most chores had to be done according to certain phases of the moon such as planting crops, weaning calves, putting eggs under setting hens and hoeing weeds in the garden. I always wished we would lose that almanac around *the time we had to hoe weeds.*

We raised lots of watermelons and dad was very strict about when we could pick them. We children couldn't wait lots of times, so we would go out and pick one and then have to bury the rinds so dad wouldn't find out. Many times, just as the watermelons were ripe, a hailstorm would come and burst the watermelons. When that happened, dad would alert the neighbors to come and get all they wanted of the busted watermelons. What the neighbors didn't want, the pigs and coyotes finished up. Coyotes love watermelons.

Margaret remembered their father's 'hot beds,' which were large holes facing south near her mother's wash house. Deep layers of manure were put into the holes beneath the soil where seeds were planted.

On sunny winter days, the hot beds were uncovered to attract the light and warmth. Whenever a hailstorm destroyed dad's crops, he would replant them with the sprouts from the hot bed.

I recall one bad hailstorm in late May when Clara and I were sent out to round up the baby chicks and turkeys. We wore ten pound buckets on our heads to protect us. The noise was deafening and our arms were black and blue when it was over. But we didn't have any lumps on our heads.

Clara and Margaret also recalled that box socials were a favorite community activity and every Sunday after church, families took turns hosting dinners to which everyone in the congregation was invited. When she graduated from high school, Clara was the only one in her graduating class. "I can have a class reunion whenever I want one," she said.

Shortly after Clara graduated from high school, a set of circumstances occurred which allowed her parents to return to Arizona and to the town they helped establish.

In January of 1931, during the height of the Great Depression, Sedona's mother, Amanda, had a deadly stroke. Sedona hurried to Gorin to care for her, but didn't arrive in time. Amanda Miller died with little left to her name, having lost everything when the Gorin bank closed down after the 'Crash.'

That same month, Carl faced one of the fiercest blizzards of the decade. He lost most of his cattle in the storm. In addition, he came down with the influenza, which was sweeping the country. For the first time in his life, Carl Schnebly took to his bed. By summer, Carl's remaining cattle broke out with the deadly anthrax disease, and Carl was forced to stay up day and night for weeks burning their carcasses, and the ground where they died, with yucca weeds. This was the only way to prevent the disease from seeping into the ground water and watering ponds. By fall, more cattle died from eating corn stalks poisoned by an early frost. Exhausted, discouraged and in poor health, Carl was forced to seek a doctor. The doctor told him he must go to a warmer, drier climate immediately or his health might be permanently impaired.

Carl sold what was left of his stock and his farm and moved the family to Phoenix where his brother William now lived. His brother Elsworth already had died in Phoenix in 1920, following an unsuccessful operation.

After three months in Phoenix, Carl couldn't resist the urge to move to Sedona, even though he'd been warned to avoid higher altitudes. Carl's old friends the Farleys (who were the first people Carl had met when he came to Arizona in 1901 and who had convinced him his possessions would be safe on the mountainside), offered him a job on their farm. So at the age of 68, Carl gratefully accepted their offer to work as a farm hand for $30 a month.

Despite his doctor's warning, Carl's health improved and he knew he would never leave Sedona again. By then there no longer was any trace of their original home, except little Pearl's grave. It was still on the land owned now by the Blacks. Carl got permission from the Cook family to move her remains to their family cemetery located off the present Airport Road. Carl carried Pearl's remains himself, and re-buried her in her present resting ground.

The Schneblys moved into a one-room frame house off the present Jordan Road and settled back into the life of their small community.

Margaret milked a cow each day for the Farleys in order to contribute a quart of milk to the family needs. Sedona washed and ironed the uniforms of the CCC (Civilian Conservation Corps) boys who worked on government jobs in and around Flagstaff and Sedona.

"Mother didn't have a washing machine," recalls Margaret. "She scrubbed those uniforms on a wash board all day, and then ironed them into the night." For this, Sedona earned about 10 cents a shirt.

Mr. Farley, who was a good carpenter, added some rooms to their little house. After Sedona stuffed newspapers and batting into the cracks to give their home more warmth, she covered the rough boards with blue and pink 'building paper.'

Then Ruth and Walter Jordan, a young couple who had taken over running the elder Jordan's fruit orchards along with their in-laws, Helen and George Jordan, hired all three Schneblys to work for them. Margaret picked fruit during harvest, Carl worked in the orchards and Sedona cleaned house, cooked, canned fruit and helped care for the Walter Jordans' three small children.

Helen Jordan reminisced about the effect of the depression on Sedona farmers in the Westerner's book, THOSE WERE THE DAYS.

During the Depression, farm prices reached a new low, and with each farmer trying to compete with the other to sell produce that you could hardly give awey, the farmers finally decided to form a cooperative. They brought their produce to our packing shed where we packed it uniformly. George did the marketing for everyone. He made regular trups each week to Cottonwood, Clarkdale, Jerome, Prescott, Flagstaff, Williams, Ashfork and Holbrook and overnight trips to Phoenix. He would get home late from these trips and we would work till midnight getting the truck loaded for the next trip the following day. Seemed like George never went to bed. He'd come in after I went to bed, take off his pants, shake them out, put them back on and head for Flagstaff.

With donated effort, the Jordans' canvas-sided packing shed soon became a packing house which today still serves the community as the Sedona Arts Center.

In the meantime, with so much grueling work

Carl and Dona in front of Sedona's old school house which later burned, 1940's.

Golden Wedding
Anniversary, 1947

Carl Schnebly, 1953

Photos courtesy of Paula Schnebly Hokanson

to be done at the Jordan farm, especially after the fall harvest, the young Jordans relied more and more on the hard-working, experienced Schneblys. In time, a strong bond and lasting friendship developed between the two couples.

Sedona, or Aunt Dona as she was affectionately called, not only endeared herself to the Jordans but to the small community as well. Aunt Dona always had a cookie jar filled with fresh baked goods for the many children who loved to visit her. She and the Jordans were active in the American Union Sunday School. Aunt Dona put herself whole-heatedly into the group, serving as their secretary-treasurer. She invested the Sunday school savings into bonds, and the group looked forward to the day when they could build a chapel where people of all denominations might worship. When the old school house, where they met, mysteriously burned down, the Assembly of God church offered their building for the use of the group. Finally, as their building fund grew, thanks to Sedona's careful investments, the Wayside Chapel was built on land donated by the Jordan family.

It was about this time, following World War II, that Hwy. 89A was completed through Oak Creek Canyon, and the first major influx of tourists began to discover the scenic wonders of the little town. Many bought property and returned later to retire. Artists, writers and other talented individuals also looked upon Sedona as the "Shangri-la of the West," and the community that Carl and Sedona helped found took on a unique personality of its own.

On February 24, 1947, Carl and Sedona celebrated their 50th wedding anniversary, and the entire community turned out to pay them homage as did old friends who traveled miles to join in the celebration. Three years later, just before the Wayside Chapel was to be dedicated on April 5, 1950, Aunt Dona was taken to the hospital for major surgery. She returned home in time for the dedication, but one month later was back in the hospital again. Carl was told that Sedona had cancer and that she only had a few months to live.

Carl disregarded the doctor's suggestion that Sedona not be told. He was no good at keeping secrets from his beloved companion of 53 years. Sedona accepted the news stoically and with her usual courage. "Everyone has to go sometime," she said, "and I'm ready."

Carl stayed constantly at Sedona's bedside, never leaving for more than a few minutes. Friends who paid daily visits were always greeted with her warm and cheerful smile.

On Sunday, November 12, 1951 the minister came to give Sedona communion. Many of her family members were at her bedside and shared in the communion ceremony. Sedona knew her time was near. She asked those present to tell everyone that rather than send flowers to her funeral, would they instead contribute to a bell for the new chapel she had helped to found. That night, the doctor, friends and family stayed with her. By 10 a.m. of the following day, Sedona Arabella Miller Schnebly died on November 13, surrounded by those she loved. She was laid to rest at the Cook family cemetery beside her darling Pearl.

Within a month, the fund for the bell for Sedona had grown substantially, fed by friends and the numerous passing tourists. Sedona's son Hank found a bell in Denver, Colorado. After a belfry was constructed by Carl and others, the new bell was constructed by Carl and others, the new bell in the wall below the belfry read:

THE WAYSIDE CHAPEL BELL
DEDICATED
IN LOVING MEMORY OF
SEDONA M. SCHNEBLY

On Mother's Day, 1951, every seat of the chapel was filled as the pastor recounted Sedona Schnebly's life story. At the end of the service, the congregation joined hands as the new bell was dedicated to the mother of the town. Carl and his son Elsworth pulled the rope together, giving the bell a voice that resounded throughout the red rock canyons Sedona M. Schnebly had grown to love so much.

Two years later, on another Mother's Day an organ also was donated in her memory. It was the last Mother's Day Carl would know. He was found slumped over his washing machine, where on March 13, 1954, he quietly slipped away at the age of 86 to join his precious lady.

Artist Susan Kliewer with
Sedona Schnebly Sculpture
*This monumental statue was
commissioned by the Sedona Red
Rocks Arts Council as the first
Art in Public Places project to
be donated to the city of Sedona.*

SEDONA "Lives" Again!

By Lisa Schnebly Heidinger

hen two strong women work together, magic is possible. Indeed, the progress being made on a monumental statue of Sedona Schnebly — appropriately, this city's first public art project — is magic in the making.

One of the strong women is the sculptor, Susan Kliewer. Living by the creek in Sedona 10 years ago, she identified with the other woman, whose name graces this small town nestled into spectacular red rocks. Sedona Schnebly had come to this land, then an untamed tangle of wilderness with only about five families scattered over the Oak Creek Canyon area, as young mother. Susan often reflects on the long days that Sedona must have put in, when working to maintain a home meant scrubbing red dust off laundry in the creek, cooking over wood she gathered herself and learning to kill snakes with a broom handle.

Susan did a different kind of work in her creek-side home; she had always been an artist, but now began unfolding in a new way — working at a foundry, she was learning to sculpt in bronze. After learning the mechanics of coating and pouring wax inside rubber molds to produce wax patterns, coating patterns with slurry to create ceramic shells, and then pouring molten bronze into the shells, Kliewer nervously embarked on her first sculpture. She asked her Navajo daughter-in-law to pose for what would become "Coin Silver," a bust of a young Navajo wearing jewelry made from old coins and pawn, items that traders called coin silver.

She later did a bronze called "Anasazi" depicting a woman of the ancient tribes who lived in the Sedona area 1,000 years ago. This piece, says Susan, came about almost effortlessly: "I felt like I let her escape from a clay piece. I didn't use a model; she just happened."

So it followed that she would begin thinking about doing another strong woman from the area's past, Sedona Schnebly.

In a bit of foreshadowing, an article in the Winter 1990 issue of "Sedona Magazine" featured Susan. In this story, author Hoyt Johnson's last question to the artist as they galloped along on horseback was about what she wanted to do next. "A monument!" she shouted, bolting ahead. "Maybe it should be of Sedona Schnebly," is Johnson's closing line to the piece.

Susan laughs when I mention this.

"Isn't that spooky?" she asks, since she's now in the final stages of the 8-foot statue of Sedona Schnebly that won her a handsome commission in competition sponsored by the Red Rock Arts Council. "I think what Hoyt wrote kind of planted the seed. Then I went to a Schnebly family reunion, and I knew I had to do the bronze." She was actually working on her first version of the statue before the arts council announced its competition for the coveted art award.

And this is where I come in. I was greatly

flattered when Susan contacted me and said that as Sedona's great-granddaughter, I bore a resemblance to the pioneer that couldn't be duplicated in straight-on photographs. She wondered if I would mind coming up to Sedona to pose, so that she could fill in the profile.

I spent a delightful day at Susan's peaceful studio-under-the-arbor while the vibrant, blond artist darted about her clay statue, reshaping the mouth, straightening a line here and there, talking as energetically as she worked. She showed me some of her other bronzes, and later, avuncular author and generally creative guy Jim Bishop came over. He assisted by taking photographs that would help Susan reconstruct the drape of a jacket sleeve, or arch of an eyebrow, later on. I loved wearing the long, denim outfit Susan brought out, and knowing that if her statue won the competition I would be able to feel that in some way, I contributed to keeping my great-grandmother's image fresh and present to a generation not yet born.

Susan may have been happier than I was when she won, but I doubt it.

Over time, the look of Susan's monumental sculpture has undergone a metamorphosis. "When you work that big, everything changes," she says. But she believes the final version of Sedona Schnebly is true to the image of the woman: "Strong, feminine, welcoming!"

She wrought the tall version of Sedona at Sedona Arts Center and is grateful, indeed, for the space they donated for her work. "They could have used the main gallery for a lot of things over the summer, but they let me work there because I needed a high ceiling," she says. "Chuck Raison, the director, was such a nice guy; all the people there made

Lisa Schnebly Hiedinger

Lisa was the model for this nine foot statue of her great-grandmother. Lisa is a professional writer and a regular columnist for the Arizona Republic.

me feel like part of the family and as it turned out, the whole community got behind my project because people were able to come by to see how it was progressing, and they brought their children to show them what it looked like."

Asked about the hardest part of her project, Susan answered, "When you work on somethig that big you can be at it all day and when you step back to inspect the progress, it doesn't look like you've done anything."

If fund raising progresses as hoped, Susan's statue will be completed by the summer of 1994. Then the community will find a place for this first piece of public art. "I hope it's in a setting where people can relax, pose for pictures and really get a chance to appreciate this artwork," Susan says wistfully. "That's happened with my large sculpture at Sinagua Plaza, and I never dreamed when I was working on it that people would be sitting on benches, taking pictures in front of it," says this delighted artist. "I hope wherever the Sedona piece goes, it's like that."

Susan has worked to imbue the statue with the qualities she admires in the woman for whom this community was named. Hospitality, gentle humor and determination are just some of the traits she's striven to communicate in this depiction of Sedona Schnebly holding a basket of apples in one hand and offering an apple in the other, outstretched hand. (Susan had considered having Sedona hold a child, as she was a mother of six and a figurative grandmother to the entire community, but decided arms already holding someone shut out the viewer, and she wanted Sedona to include, rather than exclude, people who passed by.)

There are strong similarities between the artist's

and subject's life: Susan and Sedona both had to grow up fast. Sedona became a bride on her 20th birthday, when she invoked here father's wrath by marrying Theodore Carl Schnebly, who was "the wrong religion and wouldn't amount to anything" in his new father-in-law's estimation. Sedona was written out of her parents' will for traipsing off from Missouri to the Wild West, just on the suggestion of her new brother-in-law, Daniel Ellsworth Schnebly. It was he who had first ventured out to Arizona territory and wrote in 1901 that his brother and new wife should follow him to this paradise called Oak Creek Canyon.

Theodore, who everyone called T.C., moved first, and Sedona followed by train with their 4-year-old son, Ellsworth, and 2-year-old daughter, Pearl. They had to leave their possessions piled by the train depot in Jerome and make several trips by wagon into what is now Sedona, where this young family lived in tents while their home was built.

Susan also has pioneered while raising her family. A woman who looks young enough to be a grade-school room mother, she actually is a grandmother. She used her beloved granddaughter Sacheen (daughter of her son and his Navajo wife, who posed for "Coin Silver"), as the model for a sculpture called "Little Ones," showing a child picking up a pet lamb. And like Sedona, Susan knows about the obligations associated with caring for livestock regardless of weather, dealing with property problems and living in near-isolation. She spent a year managing Marble Canyon Lodge, a remote outpost near Lee's Ferry, the Colorado River crossing above the Grand Canyon. Like Sedona Schnebly, Susan had an educated upbringing that included visits to galleries in Southern California. (Sedona studied art, elocution and music at a seminary for girls in Gorin, Missouri.)

Susan believes that time spent among Marble Canyons' red-rock towers and bluffs, with almost no company, was important for her progress as an artist. She resonates to the seclusion and timelessness of Marble Canyon so strongly that she recently purchased property there again. But she also understands that solitude magnifies pain as well as pleasure, and that Sedona Schnebly left Oak Creek and spent many years away until she was strong enough to face the almost-isolated country again.

It was not uncommon for young, pioneer women to lose children — either at childbirth, to illness or by accident — but Sedona Schnebly suffered a particularly tragic experience. She witnessed the death of her precious daughter, Pearl, when the child was dragged by her pony during an evening roundup and strangled by the reins she'd draped around her neck, in order to leave her hands free for collecting treasures like arrowheads. The pony panicked, bolted for home, and by the time Sedona and little Ellsworth got to the dooryard, hired hands had carried Pearl's beaten body into the house. (Ellsworth remembered years later picking up his sister's tiny shoe.)

After Pearl was buried in the yard by the house, the life force that had burned so brightly in Sedona seemed to fade. Anyone who has been alone near Oak Creek at night knows how the owls, rustling trees and canopy of blinking stars can create either an inspirational or foreboding mood. T.C. was told he had better leave the area that held such wrenching memories for his wife if he wanted her to survive.

There is no written record of his feelings, but

leaving this community was a big sacrifice for T.C. — financially and otherwise. His 80-acre homestead on the creek, which now is the site of Los Abrigados Resort, was to appreciate substantially. His fruit orchards were flourishing, and he had been instrumental in carving Schnebly Hill Road up the steep, eastern side of Oak Creek Canyon. Also, he had become the first postmaster of this fledgling community, which was named after Sedona when the Postmaster General rejected his first proposals, Red Rock Crossing and Schnebly Station, because the names were too long for the cancellation stamp.

However, T.C. treasured his wife. He was not a man who judged commercial success as very important compared to people. In fact, archives at Northern Arizona Uiversity showed he died with less than $500 worth of property! But what a legacy he left — in the town he helped create.

After leaving Arizona, a farm up in Boyero, Colorado, sustained T.C. and Sedona as they raised their children — Ellsworth, Genevieve, Hank, Clara and Margaret.

In later years, T.C. began to have health problems, but wouldn't quit working with his crops and livestock in rainstorms and bitter, cold temperatures. When his doctor urged him to move to the dry warmth of Phoenix, he agreed — then announced he was going back to Oak Creek Canyon instead. If he had to die, he wanted to die content.

As it turned out, T.C. regained his health after being back in the country he loved best. He and Sedona joyously joined the community where their house had once been the only lodging for visitors and newcomers. I imagine Sedona loved meeting people at church and inviting them to her home, especially since stoves weren't all wood-burning anymore and electricity was used to light the dining room, instead of candles and lanterns. The couple worked diligently to help raise money for Wayside Chapel's bell while they lived on the Jordon property at the base of Schnebly Hill Road, where T.C. did odd jobs in exchange for the living quarters on his good friend's land.

Susan Kliewer resonates to the common-sense financial considerations that were part of Sedona Schnebly's character. Though she now is a prominent artist, with work displayed at Ken Payne's prestigious galleries and people buying pieces before she's even finished with them, Susan is a woman who has been true to her passions rather than charting a path based on what would profit her financially. She understands that to fulfill your destiny, you must follow your dreams rather than a five-year plan.

So, it is justifiable that Susan has been able to bring new life to the memory of Sedona Schnebly, in the community where they both saw dreams come true. Wherever Susan may end up living, part of her will remain in Sedona, the community, just as part of Sedona, the courageous pioneer, does in the bronze statue being created out of the admiration and understanding of another strong woman.

Order
Other Thorne
Enterprises
Publications
For Your
Enjoyment

Thorne Enterprises Publications, Inc. was launched in July 1988 the successful **Experience Sedona Recreational Map.** It is the only map of the Sedona/ Oak Creek Canyon area drawn to scale and was recommended by **The Los Angeles Times (1990); Off-Road Magazine (May 1991);** and the **National Geographic Traveler (January 1992).**

Experience Sedona Recreational Map.......................................$4.95
Updated and completely revised, the new version contains a Sedona art gallery guide, a geographical column, and information on our area's new state parks, plus additional hiking, mountain bike, equestrian and off-road trails.

"With the help of a new map called EXPERIENCE SEDONA, we explored red rock trails, the Mogollon Rim and vortex areas such as Boynton Canyon, touted for having psychic energy of the levels attributed to Stonehenge and the Pyramids of Egypt. I kept this map in my car along with my map of Italy."
Judith Morgan - The Los Angeles Times

Experience Sedona Legends & Legacies...................$8.95

by Kate Ruland-Thorne

This pioneer history of Sedona by was first published in 1990 (5000 copies) and is now in it's fourth printing. Among it's many credits and rave reviews, was a recommendation by ELMER DILLS on his show in Los Angeles during their Eyewitness News feature on Sedona in 1990.* 114 Pages, 100 Illustrations, Historic map.

"More delightful than her accurate, specific information, is her choice of topics and her method of presenting them."
Lois Stalvey Sedona Red Rock News

"It's amazing that it took this many years for somebody to finally write the history of Sedona. After reading Legends and Legacies, it makes you glad nobody else tried."
Simone Butler The TAB

"Sedona's fascinating history comes alive in Legends and Legacies... an absorbing read."
The Red Rock News

The Yavapai, People of the Red Rocks........................$6.95

by Kate Ruland-Thorne

A complete history of the Yavapai people as told from their point of view. Recommended by the Ft. McDowell Yavapai Tribe. 88 Pages, 40 Historic Photos.

"The tribe has for many years had the desire to have this (book) accomplished. Now that it has been completed, I commend Kate Ruland-Thorne for a job well done."
Lois Hood
Planning coordinator
Ft. McDowell Mohave-Apache
Indian Community

White Eyes, Long Knives & Renegade Indians............$5.95

by V. Keith Thorne

The military history of General Crook's campaign against the Yavapai and Apache people of Central Arizona. 45 Pages, 20 Historic Photos, Map.

"A well researched and fascinating account of General Cook's campaign in Central Arizona."
Col. Richard Norman -U.S. Army, Retired

Experience Jerome...$6.95

by Nancy Smith & Jeanette Rhoda

"Jeanette Rodda puts the reader into the underground tunnels and vast pits of Jerome's famed copper mines and in the offices of those who built fortunes on the treasures of Cleopatra Hill. Nancy Smith's excellent research is a must for visitors to Jerome who want to understand the boom and bust foundations of this world-famous hamlet."
Bill Roberts, Editor/publisher, The Jerome Traveler

"EXPERIENCE JEROME is a professionally written book that tells how a fascinating area got to be fascinating."
James Cook, Arizona Republic

"The book is wonderful and I'm proud to be a part of it. I didn't realize Jerome and the Verde Valley was such a remarkable cleft in the world's crust. I'm very impressed and delighted to be aboard."
Rosemary De Camp, Actress born in Jerome

Screw The Golden Years $6.95
I'd rather live in the past

by V. Keith Thorne
A humorous look at growing old.

Screw The Golden Years - Book 2 ....$6.95
Oh the joys of getting old

by V. Keith Thorne
A sequel, which is even funnier than the first.

Thorne publications are available at numerous locations throughout Sedona and the state of Arizona. Distributed by Sunbelt Publications, Many Feathers, Canyonlands and Treasure Chest.

For more information or to place an order call or write:

THORNE
Enterprises
Publications, Inc.

SEDONA BOOKS & MUSIC
140 Coffee Pot Drive, Ste E-103-A
Sedona, Arizona 86336
(520) 203-0711

HOW TO ORDER

**(Add 50¢ to each additional copy for postage and handling

	No of Copies	P & H	Total
Experience Sedona Recreational Map *$4.95 + $1.25 Postage and Handling*			
Experience Sedona Legends and Legacies *$8.95 + $1.75 Postage and Handling*			
Experience Jerome and the Verde Valley *$9.95 + $2.00 Postage and Handling*			
The Yavapai People of the Red Rocks *$5.95 + $1.25 Postage and Handling*			
White Eyes, Long Knives and Renegade Indians *$4.95 + $1.25 Postage and Handling*			
Grandfather's Good Medicine *$11.95 + $2.25 Postage and Handling*			
The Legacy of Sedona Schnebly *$4.95 + $1.25 Postage and Handling*			
Wholesale Orders of 5 or More Copies Have a 40% Discount			
Tax 7% for Arizona residents only			
(checks or money orders only) **Total**			

Name _____

Address _____

_____

43